Outside and Inside
KILLER BEES

Sandra Markle

WALKER & COMPANY ❖ NEW YORK

Is this a killer bee? If it is, and if it's coming to attack you, there are likely to be lots more bees right behind it. Killer bees are a kind of honeybee. They live in a colony, or group, that works together to collect food and fight off enemies. So how can you tell if a bee is a killer bee? This book will show you.

abdomen

thorax

head

legs

Could counting the number of legs or body parts help? No, like all honeybees, killer bees are insects with six legs and three main body parts: a head, a thorax, and an abdomen.

Within a bee colony, there are three different kinds of bees: one queen bee, a few hundred male bees, called drones, and thousands of worker bees. Whether or not it's a killer bee, the bee in this photo is a worker.

Workers do a lot for their colony. Depending on its age, a worker performs different tasks. During the first week of its life as an adult, the worker cleans the comb, or wax cells the bees build for their nest. The second week the worker helps feed the developing young. Once it's about three weeks old, the worker begins producing wax flakes that emerge between the segments of its abdomen. The worker uses these flakes to build new wax cells or repair old ones. By the time it's four weeks old, the worker stops producing wax and moves on to the job of helping guard the nest entrance. Finally, once it's about five weeks old, the worker flies out to help collect nectar, which is the sweet liquid produced by flowers. It uses this to produce honey, and it continues collecting nectar and making honey for a few more weeks.

Worker bees live for only about six to eight weeks during the summer. Bees that become adults during the autumn are less active and survive the winter to help raise a new generation of workers in the spring.

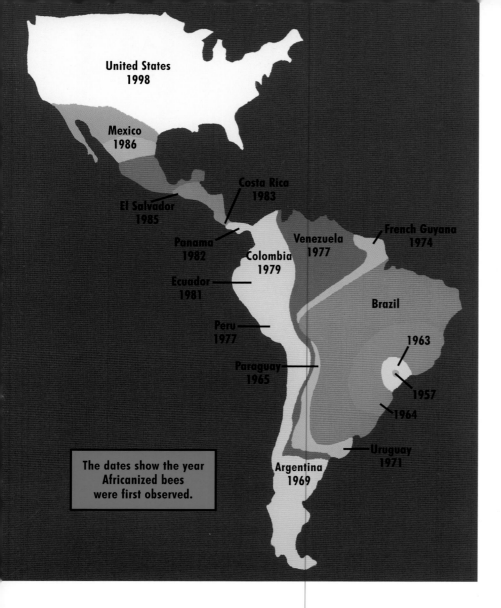

United States
1998

Mexico
1986

Costa Rica
1983

El Salvador
1985

Panama
1982

Venezuela
1977

Colombia
1979

French Guyana
1974

Ecuador
1981

Brazil

Peru
1977

1963

1957

1964

Paraguay
1965

Uruguay
1971

Argentina
1969

The dates show the year
Africanized bees
were first observed.

What most people call honeybees are European honeybees. Their ancestors lived in Europe and were brought to other parts of the world to help pollinate crops and produce honey. European honeybees in Brazil were producing less honey than expected, and researchers believed this was because of the tropical climate. In 1956, bees were imported from Africa because their native climate was similar to Brazil's. Researchers mated African queen bees with European drones in an effort to breed a bee that would produce more honey while keeping the less aggressive nature of the European bees. These new hybrids were called Africanized bees.

A year later, as researchers were testing these new hybrids' abilities, twenty-six hybrid colonies escaped into the wild. These colonies quickly grew, split up, and spread out. They even took over European-honeybee colonies, producing offspring that had the Africanized-bee traits. Look at the map to see, by color code, the path the bees followed as they spread out. The years listed show when they first appeared in each new area.

venom pouch

stinger

This bee has just stung a person. Since their escape, Africanized bees have stung and killed almost eight hundred people. That's why the Africanized bees were nicknamed killer bees. Animals are at risk too. Some farmers in South America had livestock killed by these intruders. Researchers discovered that wild animals were also attacked by the bees and sometimes moved to escape living near killer-bee nests.

It isn't that the Africanized bee's sting is more deadly. It's that more bees attack and sting at the same time. To see just how many bees would sting to defend their colony, researchers placed a leather patch in front of a killer-bee nest. Look at the results! In just this one small corner of the patch you can see how many bees are attacking, along with the white venom pouches left behind by the bees that have already stung the leather pouch. Some of the people killed by Africanized bees were stung as many as five hundred times. Africanized bees are also faster to launch an attack when disturbed. European honeybees may take as long as nineteen seconds to leave the hive. Killer bees attack in just three seconds.

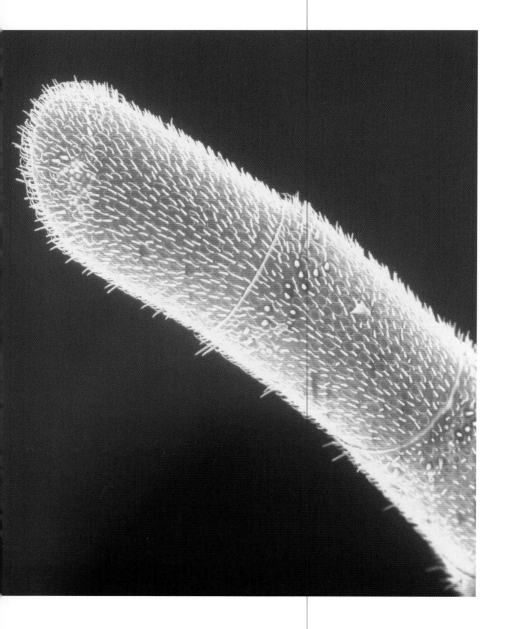

This is a bee's antenna, and it may be the reason killer bees are so quick to attack. See all of the tiny hairs on the antenna? These detect chemicals in the air that the bee interprets as scents. One of the scents a bee picks up is the colony's alarm scent, which some people report smells like ripe bananas.

A bee's antennas are like two long noses that move through the air, picking up scents. A bee's sense of smell is also so keen it can detect scents as much as one hundred times weaker than you can smell. So these guard bees will sense an intruder well before it reaches the colony. An Africanized bee's antennas are even more sensitive than those of European honeybees. However, the antennas of both kinds of bees look the same. So looking at a bee's antennas won't help you identify a killer bee.

antennas

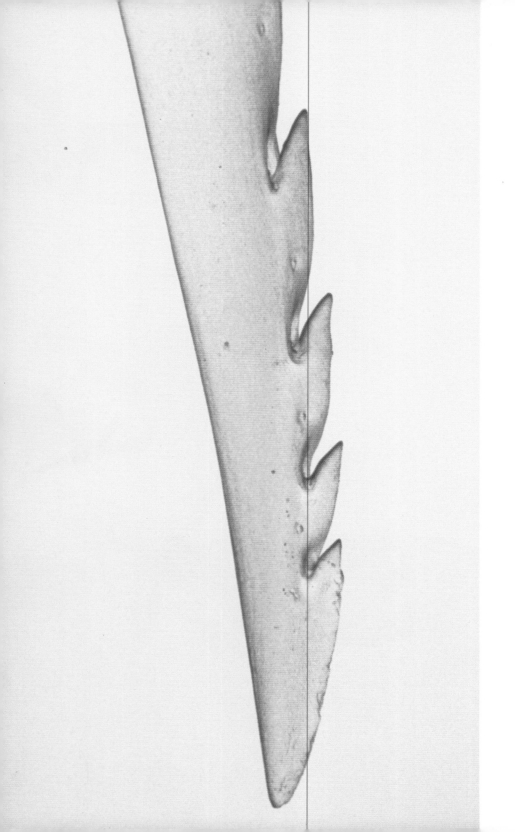

Neither will looking at its stinger. This magnified view lets you see that the bee's stinger has backward-curving barbs like those on a fishhook. Both Africanized- and European-honeybee workers have stingers with this same sort of barbed tip. Tiny as a pin, the stinger is retracted into the bee's abdomen until needed. To attack, the bee pushes its stinger into its enemy's skin. Then a muscular pouch filled with venom contracts, injecting this poison through the stinger's hollow shaft. Because the barbs make the stinger stick, the venom pouch rips out when the bee moves, killing the bee. (You can see that on page 7.) So a worker bee can sting only once. The queen bee has a smooth stinger and can sting more than once, but queens usually only attack other queen bees when fighting to take over a colony. Drones lack a stinger.

big
eyes

small
eyes

What about a bee's eyes? Could they help you identify a killer bee? No, all honeybees have five eyes, two big and three small. The small eyes just detect light. They help the bee figure out in which direction it's flying based on where the sun is in the sky. The two big eyes enable the bee to see its world.

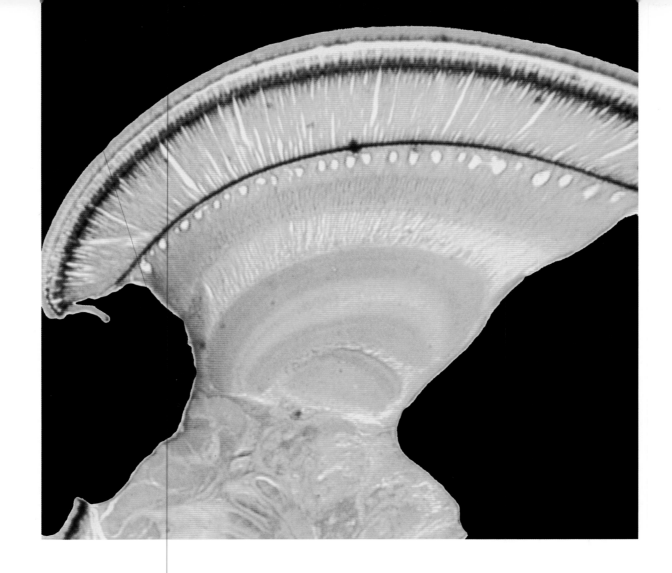

This special picture taken through a microscope lets you peek inside one of a bee's big eyes. What looks like stripes topped with dark dots are separate eye units. Each of your eyes has a single lens and layer of light-sensitive cells. A bee's big eyes may have more than six thousand separate units, each with its own lens and light-sensitive cells. Researchers believe the bee's brain pieces together messages from all of these eye units to produce an image.

Because researchers believe a bee's view of the world is made up of lots of colored dots instead of solid shapes, a bee's vision probably isn't as sharp as yours. But a bee is quicker to detect when something moves. Each of a bee's eye units updates the brain at least one hundred times a second. Human eyes only update the brain about twenty times a second. Having more updates may help a bee judge where to land when a flower is waving in the wind.

Researchers also believe bees can see ultraviolet (UV) light, a kind of light humans can't see. When viewed with UV-sensitive film, as shown in the image on the right, researchers discovered flowers have special markings that show up only in that light. These markings may guide bees to the flower's supply of nectar.

As bees travel from flower to flower in search of nectar, they also spread the flower's pollen grains, or reproductive cells. This makes it possible for the flower to produce seeds that will grow into new plants. And that brings up another reason people don't like killer bees.

Some plants, like apple and olive trees, need to have bees carry the pollen between their flowers to produce fruit. At just the right time, beekeepers move hives of European honeybees to where they are needed. Later, the colonies are trapped inside their hives and transported to where they can pollinate another crop. If moved, a colony of killer bees would be just as likely to fly away as stick with their hive. Then crops wouldn't get pollinated, and the beekeepers would be out of business.

Africanized bees also store less honey than European honeybees. In their home range, they didn't need to store much food. It was always warm, and plants were always in bloom. So when one food supply started to fade, the colony simply moved on.

But could you tell by tasting a colony's honey whether it had been made by killer bees? No, the honey's flavor is affected by the kind of flower it comes from. All honeybees produce honey the same way.

Here's how honey is made. First, a bee sucks nectar into its crop, a storage sac. There the nectar is mixed with special digestive juices that change the nectar into honey. Next, the bee passes the honey onto another bee. Look closely and you'll see the drop of honey being transferred between the two bees. Just as your tongue dries quickly when you stick it out, exposing honey to the air helps it become less watery. Finally, when enough water has been removed, honey becomes the familiar gooey, golden liquid.

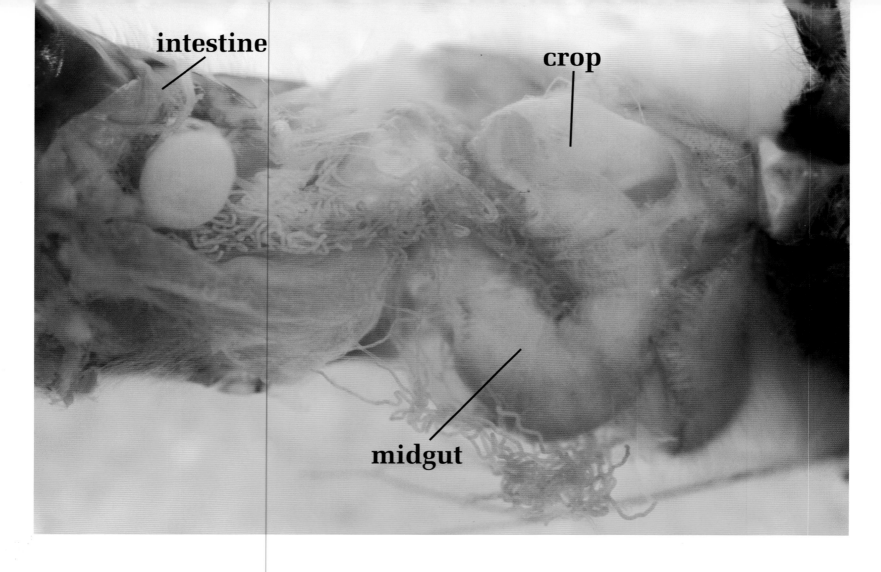

intestine

crop

midgut

Whether it has been stored or is freshly made, honey is a bee's main food supply. When a bee needs food, a valve lets some of the honey that entered its crop move into its midgut, where special juices start to break down the food. Next, the food moves into the tubelike intestine. There, more juices break it into nutrients, chemicals the bee's body can use. These nutrients pass through the walls of the intestine and into the blood. Then the heart, a muscular tube, pumps the blood through spaces to all of the bee's body parts.

spiracles

Besides food, bees also need oxygen, one of the gases in the air. So a bee's body has holes, called spiracles, in its sides to let air enter air sacs. It needs these holes because its body has a tough armorlike covering. From the air sacs, oxygen passes into a network of tubes that stretch throughout the bee's body. When oxygen combines with nutrients to produce energy, a waste gas, carbon dioxide, is given off. This waste gas travels back to the air sacs and escapes through the spiracles.

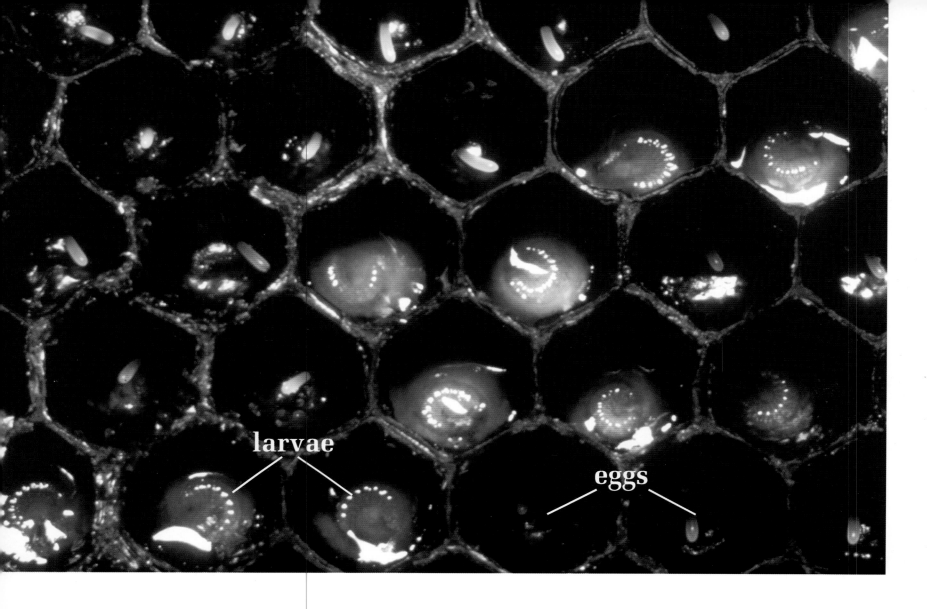

larvae

eggs

These are honeybee eggs and larvae. Like all bees, killer bees go through three stages as they develop: egg; larva, the stage that needs to be fed; and pupa, the stage that changes into an adult. (You will see the pupa on page 28.)

Could you tell a killer-bee colony by the way the workers care for the brood of developing young?

European honeybees

Africanized honeybees

Yes, you could if the nest was disturbed. European honeybees cling to the brood cells to defend the young. Africanized bees run away and cluster together to defend themselves.

Africanized honeybees also do something else European honeybees don't do. They migrate. This means that the whole colony leaves the nest and moves to a new location. Killer bees migrate when workers have trouble finding a supply of nectar or when their nest is disturbed.

However, it's common for both killer bees and European honeybees to swarm, which is when the colony splits into two groups: one that stays in the old nest with a new queen and one that leaves to build a new nest with the old queen. Swarming often happens in the spring, when a nest becomes crowded and lots of food is available. Swarming leaves part of the colony with a food supply that was stored up by the bigger group. Since killer bees don't store much honey, it's just as likely that the whole colony will move. That way there will be more workers at the new site to start bringing home food.

pupae

Africanized bees behave very differently when they get ready to migrate than they do when they swarm. Since no one will be left behind, the colony waits for the pupae to emerge as adults. Next, the workers eat whatever food has been stored up. They also eat the larvae. These young would soon die anyway, since no workers would be left to feed them. And eating the larvae gives the workers the extra energy they will need for a long flight.

queen bee

Whether migrating or swarming, it takes two to three weeks for the queen bee to get ready to fly. She is just naturally a bigger bee than the workers. She's also heavy with eggs, too heavy for a long flight. But when the workers stop feeding her, the queen stops producing eggs and slims down.

Once the colony is ready to migrate, or split up to swarm, some of the workers perform a waggle dance. This means they circle and vibrate their abdomen. This lets the other bees know in which direction to travel. No one knows yet how the bees choose a direction.

When the traveling colony finally settles in a new area, workers fly off in search of a new nest site. Returning scouts perform a waggle dance to signal the direction and distance to the possible nest site. Once a number of scouts report on the same site, the colony moves there.

Next, workers produce wax and begin building the new comb. The queen once again lays eggs. Other workers nurse the developing young, and soon new workers begin to emerge. The colony is growing bigger again.

Eventually, the colony will grow big enough to split. Africanized-honeybee colonies split more often than European colonies, as often as six times a year.

A European-honeybee colony is at risk of being taken over by killer bees any time it is queenless, such as when part of the colony leaves with the old queen. At that time, the new queen that will take over the remaining part of the colony may not yet have emerged. Sometimes, small swarms of Africanized bees invade such queenless European colonies. Then the killer-bee queen takes over, killing any developing queens and producing young with killer-bee traits.

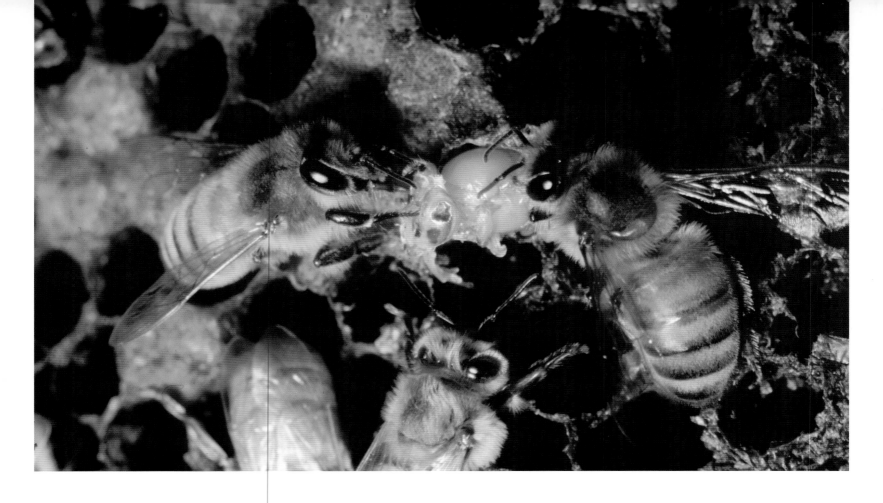

There is also a way killer bees can invade European colonies without attacking. If killer-bee colonies are nearby, a new European queen may mate with a killer-bee male. Then the workers the European queen produces will have killer-bee traits. So will some of the new queens she produces. And one of the traits of killer-bee queens is to go through the larva and pupa stages faster than European queens. Since the first queen to emerge as an adult kills her still-developing rivals, the killer-bee queen takes over the colony. Here you can see the workers cleaning up by eating the remains of the dead bees. The killer-bee queen's offspring will all have killer-bee traits.

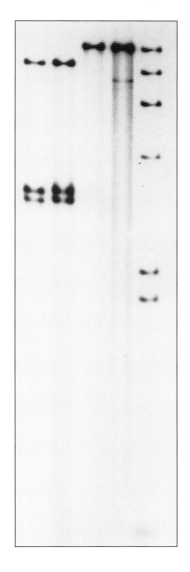

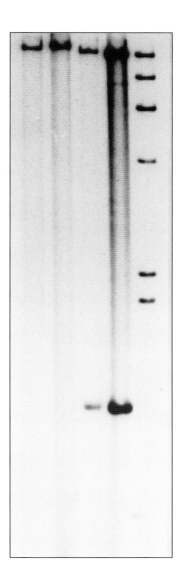

European honeybee DNA   **Africanized honeybee DNA**

Was the honeybee on page 2 a killer bee?   The only sure way to identify a killer bee is to check its DNA, the chemical code that determines its traits.   But checking a bee's DNA requires training and special equipment.   So how can you tell if a honeybee is a killer bee?

You probably can't tell just by looking at a bee. You would need to observe its behavior and that of its colony over time. The bee on page 2 is a European honeybee. The bee on this page is a killer bee. Compare the two for yourself.

People are learning how to live with and control killer bees. Some researchers are trying to find a way to block killer bees from sensing the alarm scent that triggers an attack. Others are trying to find ways to prevent killer bees from taking over European-honeybee colonies.

Everyone wonders how far the killer bees will spread. So far, long, cold winters seem to be limiting the spread of the Africanized bees in North America. But no one knows if that will continue to be true. How harmful the killer bees' effect will be on farming and honey production, and even whether people can learn to safely live with them, remains to be seen.

Glossary/Index

Words that appear in red in the text are included in the glossary.

A special pronunciation guide has been added with each entry to help readers sound out the words.

ABDOMEN   *AB-duh-mun*   The body segment that contains organs that digest food, produce wax, and sting. **4, 5, 12, 30**

ANTENNA   *an-TEN-a*   A movable body part attached to the head. It contains scent-sensitive cells. **10–11**

BLOOD   *blud*   The fluid that carries food and oxygen to all the body parts and carries wastes away. **22**

BRAIN   *brayn*   The central body part that receives and analyzes messages about what is happening inside and outside the body. The brain sends instructions to put the body into action. **14–15**

BROOD   *brood*   The developing young. **24–25**

CARBON DIOXIDE   *KAR-bun die-OX-seyed*   A waste gas given off naturally during activity. **23**

COLONY   *KAH-luh-nee*   All of the bees living and working together to make food, produce young, and defend themselves. **3, 5, 6, 9–12, 19–20, 24, 27–28, 30, 33–34, 37**

COMB   *kome*   The wax cells that form the bee's nest, where the brood develop and food is stored. **5, 33**

CROP   *krop*   A saclike body part that stretches to let the bee store nectar and carry it home to the hive. **21–22**

DRONE   *drone*   A male bee. **5–6, 12**

EGG   *eg*   The first stage of development in bees. **24, 29, 33**

EYE   *ii*   The body part that detects light and color and sends signals to the brain, where they are analyzed. **13–16**

HEAD   *hed*   The body segment that contains the brain, antennas, mouthparts, and eyes. **4–5**

HEART   *hart*   An open-ended tube that keeps blood flowing through the spaces inside a bee's body. **22**

HIVE   *hiiv*   The name given to a place where a bee colony makes its nest. It is also another name for a colony of bees. **9, 19**

HONEY   *HUH-nee*   The sweet food produced and stored by bees. It is made from nectar. **5–6, 20–22, 27, 37**

HYBRID   *HI-brid*   An animal that results from the mating of two parents from two different species of the same kind of animal. **6**

INSECT   *IN-sekt*   A kind of animal with six legs and three main body parts: head, thorax, and abdomen. Bees are insects. **5**

INTESTINE   *in-TES-tun*   The body part where special juices finish breaking food down into nutrients. **22**

LARVA   *LAR-vuh*   The feeding stage of developing bees. **24, 28, 34**

MIGRATE   *MII-graat*   The process in which the entire bee colony leaves to start a new nest. **27–30**

NECTAR   *NEK-ter*   The sweet liquid produced by flowers to attract bees. **5, 16–17, 21, 27**

NUTRIENTS   *NOO-tree-ntz*   The chemicals into which food is broken down. When combined with oxygen, food nutrients produce the energy needed for use by the bee's body to live and be active. **22–23**

OXYGEN   *AHK-sih-jen*   A gas in the air that passes into the bees's blood through the spiracles. The blood then carries the oxygen through the bee's body, where it is combined with nutrients to release energy. **23**

POLLEN   *PAH-lun*   The grains produced by flowers as part of their reproductive process. When combined with egg cells, seeds form. Bees carry pollen grains from flower to flower. They also use some pollen for food. **17, 19**

PUPA   *PYOO-puh*   The stage in which the larva is transformed into an adult. **24, 28, 34**

QUEEN   *kween*   A female bee capable of producing new workers and drones for the colony. She may live for several years. **5–6, 12, 27, 29, 33–34**

SCENT   *sent*   The special chemicals that bees detect and give off to find food, work together, and signal the need to attack. **10–11, 37**

SPIRACLE   *SPEAR-i-kul*   A hole in a bee's tough body covering to let oxygen in and carbon dioxide out. **23**

STING   *sting*   The injection of venom by a bee into an enemy. **7, 9, 12**

SWARM   *sworm*   The process in which part of the bee colony leaves with the old queen to start a new nest. The remaining workers support the newly emerged queen. **27–30, 33**

THORAX   *THOR-aks*   The body segment that contains the bee's legs and wings. **4, 5**

ULTRAVIOLET (UV) LIGHT   *ul-truh-VII-uh-lut (you vee) liit*   Light rays that can be detected by bees but not by humans. **16**

VENOM   *VE-num*   A poisonous substance produced in the bee's abdomen, stored in a pouch, and injected through a hollow stinger. **12**

WAX   *waks*   A material produced by worker bees during part of their life. The workers chew this substance and shape it into the cells that form the cells in the comb. **5, 33**

WORKER   *WUR-kur*   A female bee that is not capable of producing any young. She lives about six weeks, helping to raise new worker bees, defending the colony, and collecting food. **5, 12, 24, 27–30, 33–34**

For good friends Tim and Trish Coleman

First published in the United States of America in 2004 by
Walker Publishing Company, Inc.

Published simultaneously in Canada by Fitzhenry and Whiteside, Markham, Ontario L3R 4T8

For information about permission to reproduce selections from this book, write to Permissions, Walker & Company, 104 Fifth Avenue, New York, New York 10011

Library of Congress Cataloging-in-Publication Data

Markle, Sandra.
Outside & inside killer bees / Sandra Markle.
p. cm.
ISBN 0-8027-8906-4 (HC) — ISBN 0-8027-8907-2 (RE)
1. Africanized honeybee—Juvenile literature. I. Title: Outside and inside killer bees. II. Title.

QL568.A6.M52 2004
595.79'9—dc22
2003070500

Book design by Victoria Allen

Visit Walker & Company's Web site at www.walkeryoungreaders.com

Printed in Hong Kong

2 4 6 8 10 9 7 5 3 1

Acknowledgments: The author would like to thank Peter Johns, research fellow in Entomology at Canterbury Museum, Christchurch, New Zealand; Dr. Stanley Schneider, professor of biology at the University of North Carolina, Charlotte; and Dr. Gloria DeGrandi-Hoffman, research leader, Carl Hayden Bee Research Center, Tucson, Arizona, for sharing their expertise and enthusiasm. Finally, a special thanks to Skip Jeffery, who shared the effort and joy of creating this book.

Note to Parents and Teachers: The books in the Outside and Inside series enable young readers to discover how different animals are uniquely suited to survive. Kids investigate the physical features and behaviors that cause these animals to be successful in their particular environment.

Photo Credits

Cover: courtesy of Edward Ross
Page 1:   courtesy of Edward Ross
Page 2:   courtesy of Ken Preston Mafham
Page 4:   courtesy of Edward Ross
Page 6:   map: courtesy of Sandra Markle/data provided by Dr. Gloria DeGrandi-Hoffman
Page 7:   courtesy of Ken Lorenzen
Page 8:   courtesy of Ken Lorenzen
Page 9:   courtesy of Anita Collins, U.S. Department of Agriculture
Page 10:   courtesy of Robbin Thorp and R. O. Schuster

Page 11:   courtesy of Ken Lorenzen
Page 12:   courtesy of Robbin Thorpe
Page 13:   courtesy of Ken Lorenzen
Page 14:   courtesy of Randolf Menzel
Page 15:   courtesy of Skip Jeffery
Page 16:   courtesy of Randolf Menzel
Page 17:   courtesy of Edward Ross
Page 18:   courtesy of Skip Jeffery
Page 19:   courtesy of Skip Jeffery
Page 20:   courtesy of Ken Lorenzen
Page 21:   courtesy of Edward Ross
Page 22:   courtesy of Simon Pollard

Page 23:   courtesy of Simon Pollard
Page 24:   courtesy of Ken Lorenzen
Page 25:   (top and bottom): courtesy of Dr. Gloria DeGrandi-Hoffman
Page 26:   courtesy of Edward Ross
Page 28:   courtesy of Ken Lorenzen
Page 29:   courtesy of Stanley Schneider
Page 31:   courtesy of Ken Lorenzen
Page 32:   courtesy of Ken Lorenzen
Page 34:   courtesy of Ken Lorenzen
Page 35:   courtesy of Deborah Smith
Page 36:   courtesy of Stanley Schneider

MAY 2005